I0149334

The Kingdom Capitalist

Building Wealth for the Great Commission

Jason Kokenzie

Set Free INC

About the Author

Jason Kokenzie is a Kingdom entrepreneur, pastor, and mentor dedicated to helping believers bridge the gap between financial survival and spiritual significance. As the author of The Kingdom Capitalist and founder of iteachfreedom.com, Jason challenges the traditional "9-to-5 constraint," teaching others how to buy back their time for ministry through strategic asset building. A seasoned church planter with a passion for revitalization across the United States, he leverages his extensive background in real estate, online business, and business acquisitions to prove that the marketplace is not a distraction from the Gospel, but one of its most powerful platforms. Jason empowers "Kingdom Capitalists" to view wealth as a weapon for the Great Commission. His philosophy centers on the "Multiplication Mandate"—the idea that financial freedom is the fuel for radical flexibility, allowing believers to fund missions, mentor the next generation, and follow the Holy Spirit's lead without a boss's permission. A husband and father of four, Jason's mission is to raise up a generation of lenders who can populate heaven by making their money serve the Master.

PlantFaith.com

ITeachFreedom.com

JasonKokenzie.com

The information provided in this book is for educational and informational purposes only. The contents of this book should not be considered as financial, legal, or investment advice. The author and publisher are not liable for any losses or damages that may result from the use of the information contained herein. Readers are encouraged to consult with a qualified professional before making any financial decisions.

Published by:
Set Free INC

jasonkokenzie.com

Printed in the United States of America

Contents

Introduction: The Forgotten Tool of the Kingdom

We often treat the intersection of faith and finance with deep suspicion. Inside the church, we hear the warning that "the love of money is the root of all evil," but in our minds, we frequently shorten it to "money is the root of all evil."

This subtle shift in thinking has created a paralysis in the body of Christ. Many believers live with a low-level sense of financial guilt. We worry that having a surplus is a sign of a spiritual deficit. We fear that pursuing business success might distract us from our "real" ministry. As a result, we often leave one of the most powerful tools for Kingdom expansion sitting on the table.

This booklet exists to explore a different paradigm: that capital, when placed in the hands of a disciplined disciple, becomes one of the most potent weapons for fulfilling the Great Commission.

This is not a call to serve money. It is a call to make money serve the Master.

A New Perspective on Stewardship

If we want to see a massive shift in how we reach the lost, we must change how we view our resources. Scripture is not silent on this. In Luke 16:9, Jesus gives a directive that shocks many modern readers: "I tell you, use worldly wealth to gain friends for yourselves, so that when it is gone, you will be welcomed into eternal dwellings."

Jesus is telling us to take something temporary—money—and exchange it for something eternal—souls.

This is the heart of the **Kingdom Capitalist**. It is not about hoarding wealth for comfort or status. It is about generating resources to fuel the mission. 1 Timothy 6:17-19 instructs those with means not to be arrogant, but to be "rich in good deeds" and "generous and willing to share." When we view wealth through this lens, business and investing cease to be "secular" activities. They become acts of spiritual warfare.

The Kingdom Multiplier Effect

Throughout these pages, we will walk through a strategy to align your financial life with your spiritual calling. We will look at the principle of multiplication found in 2 Timothy 2:2, where Paul instructs Timothy to entrust the gospel to reliable people who will teach others.

We usually apply this verse to teaching, but it applies to stewardship as well. We will explore how business, passive income, and intentional asset management create a "Kingdom Multiplier" effect. When you break free from the constraints of trading time for money, you gain the freedom to disciple others, fund church plants, and support missionaries in ways you never thought possible.

We will cover three main ideas:

1. **Business as Mission:** How the marketplace is a primary vehicle for discipleship, not a distraction from it.

2. **Passive Income as Freedom:** How decoupling your income from your time allows you to be fully available for the work of the ministry.

3. **Intentional Stewardship:** moving from a defensive posture of hoarding to an offensive posture of expanding the Kingdom.

Your Invitation

You may have felt a tension in your spirit for years—a desire to do big things for God, but a limitation in your bank account or your schedule. You want to give more, go more, and serve more, but the demands of bills and debt hold you back.

It is time to break that cycle.

Whether you are deep in debt, just starting a business, or managing significant assets, the principles here are for you. We are going to challenge the culture of safety and replace it with a culture of stewardship. We are going to move from financial guilt to financial peace through faith.

Welcome to the journey of the Kingdom Capitalist. Let's get to work.

Chapter 1: The Theology of "Unrighteous Mammon"

Theme: Money is neutral; usage is spiritual.
Scripture Focus: Luke 16:9

If you grew up in church, you've likely heard a sermon on the Parable of the Shrewd Manager found in Luke 16. It is one of the most confusing stories Jesus ever told.

In the story, a manager is about to get fired for wasting his master's possessions. Panicked about his future, he decides to secure his retirement by making friends with his master's debtors. He calls them in one by one and slashes their debts. "You owe 800 gallons of olive oil? Make it 400. You owe 1,000 bushels of wheat? Make it 800."

It sounds like fraud. It sounds dishonest. And yet, when the master finds out, he doesn't have the manager arrested. He *commends* him for being shrewd.

Then Jesus drops the hammer with verse 9:

"I tell you, use worldly wealth to gain friends for yourselves, so that when it is gone, you will be welcomed into eternal dwellings." (Luke 16:9, ESV)

This verse is the cornerstone of the Kingdom Capitalist mindset. Jesus calls money "worldly wealth" (or in the King James, "unrighteous mammon"). He acknowledges that money is part of this fallen world system. But he does not say to avoid it. He does not say to burn it. He says to *use* it.

Specifically, use it to invest in friendships that last a lifetime.

The Weapon, Not the Enemy

For too long, the enemy has convinced the church that money is radioactive. We treat it like something we should handle as little as possible. We quote 1 Timothy 6:10, "For the love of money is a root of all kinds of evils. It is through this craving that some have wandered away from the faith and pierced themselves with many pangs.", "For the love of money is a root of all kinds of evil," but we functionally live as if *money itself* is the root of evil.

This creates a dangerous poverty theology. We begin to believe that being broke is holy and being wealthy is suspect.

But consider a brick. Is a brick evil? If I throw it through a window, it's a tool of destruction. If I use it to build an orphanage, it's a tool of shelter. The brick has no soul; it has no morality. It takes on the character of the hand that holds it.

Money is a brick.

When you, a disciple of Jesus, hold capital in your hands, that capital is sanctified by your intent. If your intent is to impress your neighbors with a luxury car, that money has become an idol. But if your intent is to fund a church plant, support a missionary family, or free a single mom from debt, that money has become a weapon of righteousness.

Kingdom Venture Capital

In the business world, Venture Capitalists (VCs) are investors who pour money into startups they believe will change the world (and make a return). They look for high-impact opportunities.

As believers, we need to start viewing our bank accounts as funds for **Kingdom Venture Capital**.

When Jesus says to use worldly wealth to "gain friends," he isn't talking about buying popularity. He is talking about souls. Who are the "friends" who will welcome you into eternal dwellings? They are the people who are in heaven because you funded the mission that reached them.

Imagine arriving in heaven and being greeted by a stranger who says, "You don't know me, but your business profits paid for the Bibles that were sent to my village. Because of your faithfulness to steward wealth, I am here."

That is the ROI (Return on Investment) of the Kingdom.

This shifts the entire conversation from "How much can I keep?" to "How much can I deploy?"

Breaking the Spirit of Financial Guilt

Many of you reading this feel a low-grade guilt whenever you make money. You might feel bad about asking for a raise, charging a fair price for your services, or wanting to get out of debt. You've been taught that spiritual people shouldn't care about money.

This mindset cripples the Great Commission.

If the church is broke, who funds the mission? If every Christian is drowning in consumer debt, barely making minimum payments, who has the surplus to help the widow and the orphan?

Poverty is not a fruit of the spirit. Neither is greed. The fruit we are looking for is *faithfulness*.

God does not need your money—He owns the cattle on a thousand hills. But He uses your money to train your heart. If you can be trusted with "unrighteous mammon" (money), He will trust you with true riches (spiritual authority).

We must stop apologizing for being productive. We must stop feeling guilty for seeking profit, provided that profit is gained honestly and used for God's glory.

The Strategy: How to Shift Your Mindset

So, how do we move from a poverty mindset to a stewardship mindset?

1. Stop calling it "My Money."
This is the first step of discipleship. Psalm 24:1 says, "The earth is the Lord's and the fullness thereof, the world and those who dwell therein." says, "The earth is the Lord's, and everything in it." You are not the owner; you are the money manager. If you work for a company and manage their budget, you don't stress about spending it on the company's goals because it's not your money. It's the same with God. Ask Him, "Lord, how do you want your funds allocated this month?"

2. Attack Debt as a Spiritual Enemy.
Debt is not just a financial problem; it is a spiritual shackle. Proverbs 22:7 says, "The rich rules over the poor, and the borrower is the slave of the lender" tells us the borrower is slave to the lender. You cannot be fully free to follow Jesus wherever He leads if Visa and Mastercard own your future. Getting out of debt isn't just about math; it's about buying back your freedom to serve the King.

3. Set a "Finish Line" for Your Lifestyle.

The world says as your income increases, your lifestyle should increase. Kingdom Capitalists say as income increases, *giving* should increase. Decide how much is "enough" for your family to live reasonably and generously. Anything above that line is Kingdom Venture Capital waiting to be deployed.

Conclusion

Money is a temporary tool for an eternal job. It will burn up in the end. It has no value in heaven—unless you send it ahead of you by investing in people.

Don't fear money. Don't love money. Master it.

Make it work for the only thing that matters: the expansion of the Kingdom of God.

Chapter 2: The Business of Discipleship

Theme: Business as a vehicle for the Great Commission.
Scripture Focus: 2 Timothy 2:2

There is a wall that exists in the minds of many believers. On one side of the wall is the "Sacred." This is where we put Sunday mornings, Bible studies, mission trips, and prayer meetings. On the other side of the wall is the "Secular." This is where we put our jobs, our businesses, our contracts, and our profit margins.

We have been conditioned to believe that the "Secular" is a necessary evil—something we do just to pay the bills so we can get back to the "Sacred" work of ministry.

But what if that wall is an illusion? What if the marketplace isn't a distraction from ministry, but actually one of the most effective platforms for it?

When Paul wrote to his young protégé Timothy, he gave him a blueprint for how the Kingdom expands. He wrote:

"and what you have heard from me in the presence of many witnesses entrust to faithful men, who will be able to teach others also." (2 Timothy 2:2)

This is the multiplication mandate. Paul taught Timothy. Timothy teaches faithful men. Faithful men teach others. It creates a chain reaction of discipleship.

For centuries, we have assumed this verse only applies to pastors training other pastors. But the principles of 2 Timothy 2:2—mentorship, delegation, and multiplication—are the exact same principles that drive successful businesses.

The Proximity of the Workplace

Why is business such a powerful tool for discipleship? The answer is simple: **Proximity.**

In a traditional church model, a pastor might see his congregation for two or three hours a week. He sees them when they are wearing their "Sunday best," smiling, and hiding their problems.

In a business, you see people for 40 hours a week. You see them when they are stressed. You see them when a project fails. You see them when they are struggling with their marriage or their finances. You are in the trenches with them.

Discipleship is not a class; it is a relationship. Jesus didn't just lecture the disciples; He lived with them. He traveled with them. He ate with them.

The marketplace provides the "life-on-life" environment that is required for deep spiritual growth. As a business owner or a manager, you have a captive audience. You have the authority to influence the culture of your team. You have the opportunity to model Christ-like character in high-pressure situations.

The Three Models of Kingdom Business

How do we actually apply 2 Timothy 2:2 in a commercial setting? We can look at three distinct models.

1. The Business Model: Culture as Evangelism

Your business culture is your testimony. If you put a fish symbol on your business card but treat your employees poorly, you are doing more damage to the Gospel than a staunch atheist.

However, if you build a business based on Kingdom values—integrity, excellence, generosity, and service—you create a gravitational pull. People are drawn to light. When employees see a boss who admits mistakes, who serves the team rather than ruling over them, and who prioritizes people over profit, they start asking questions. They start wondering *why* you are different.

That curiosity is the open door for the Gospel.

2. The Mentorship Model: spiritual parenting

This is the heart of 2 Timothy 2:2. In business, we call it "professional development" or "coaching." In the Kingdom, we call it discipleship.

Imagine taking a young employee under your wing. You teach them how to do the job, yes. But you also teach them how to handle conflict biblically. You teach them the value of hard work as an act of worship. You mentor them on how to manage their finances so they aren't enslaved by debt.

You are "entrusting to faithful men" the skills of life and the truths of Scripture simultaneously. You are helping them grow up—not just as workers, but as human beings made in the image of God.

3. The Resource Model: Fueling the Fire

Finally, business is the engine that funds the mission. We often look at the early church in Acts and marvel at their generosity. They sold land and possessions to make sure no one had need.

Today, business owners have the unique capacity to generate the surplus needed for this kind of work. When your business is profitable, you don't just buy a bigger boat. You fund a church plant. You support an orphanage. You provide the seed capital for a young family trying to adopt.

Profit is not the end goal; profit is the fuel for the Great Commission.

Breaking the "Full-Time Ministry" Myth

One of the most damaging lies in the modern church is the idea that "Full-Time Ministry" refers only to people who draw a paycheck from a church budget.

If you are a Christian, you are in full-time ministry. Period.

If you are a plumber, your van is your pulpit. If you are an accountant, your desk is your altar. If you are a CEO, your boardroom is your mission field.

We need to stop waiting for "professional Christians" to do the work of ministry. The pastors are there to "equip the saints for the work of ministry" (Ephesians 4:12). You are the saint. The marketplace is the work.

Practical Steps for the Kingdom Capitalist

If you want to turn your work into a platform for discipleship, start here:

1. Pray for your "Timothy."
Ask God to show you one person in your workplace who is a "person of peace"—someone who is open, hungry, and faithful. You don't need to preach to the whole company tomorrow. Just find one person to pour into.

2. Redefine Success.

Look at your P&L (Profit and Loss) statement. It tells you if you are making money. But what is your spiritual P&L? Are people growing? Are employees feeling valued? Is the atmosphere filled with anxiety or peace? Start measuring success by the lives you impact, not just the revenue you generate.

3. Be Excellent.

This cannot be overstated. You earn the right to speak into someone's life by being good at what you do. If you are lazy, incompetent, or disorganized, no one will care about your theology. Excellence builds the platform; the Gospel is the message.

Conclusion

Business is not a necessary evil. It is a holy calling. It is the mechanism by which we bring order out of chaos, provide for our neighbors, and create the relational bridges necessary to share the hope of Jesus.

Do not leave your faith in the parking lot on Monday morning. Bring it into the building. The Kingdom of God is open for business.

Chapter 3: The 9-to-5 Constraint

Theme: Moving from "Trading Time for Money" to "Buying Back Time."

We live in a culture that treats the 40-hour work week as a moral imperative. From the time we are in school, we are trained to sit in rows, follow instructions, ring a bell, and move to the next task. We are groomed to be employees.

There is nothing inherently sinful about having a job. Labor is biblical; Adam had a job in the Garden before the Fall. But we must be honest about the structural limitations of the modern "9-to-5" system when it comes to the Great Commission.

The fundamental flaw of the employee model is this: **You are trading your life's finite hours for a fixed paycheck.**

This is a linear equation. If you work 40 hours, you get paid for 40 hours. If you stop working, the money stops flowing. While this provides a certain level of security, it imposes a hard ceiling on your Kingdom impact.

The Ceiling on Availability

Imagine your pastor calls you on a Tuesday morning. "There is a crisis in a family down the street. The father just left, the mother is devastated, and they need someone to sit with them, pray with them, and help them navigate this mess. Can you go?"

If you are in the 9-to-5 trap, your answer is likely, "I wish I could, but I have a meeting at 10:00 AM. I can go after 5:00 PM."

By 5:00 PM, the immediate crisis has shifted. The opportunity for that specific ministry moment has passed.

When you sell your time to an employer, you are no longer the master of your schedule. You have sold your availability. You might have a heart for missions, but if you only get two weeks of vacation a year, your ability to go to the nations is dictated by a corporate HR policy, not the Holy Spirit.

We must recognize that the "Industrial Age" mindset—working for 40 years to get a gold watch and a pension—often hinders the "Apostolic" mindset of rapid expansion and mobility.

The Employee Trap vs. The Kingdom Entrepreneur

This is not about disparaging hard work. It is about efficiency.

In the **Employee Trap**, you are the asset. If you get sick, the asset is broken, and income stops. If you want to give more to the church, you have to work more hours or hope for a raise. You are limited by your own physical capacity.

The **Kingdom Entrepreneur** thinks differently. They don't want to *be* the asset; they want to *own* assets.

An asset is something that works whether you are there or not. A business with systems, a rental property, a dividend-paying stock portfolio—these are soldiers that fight for you while you sleep.

Why does this matter for the Gospel?

Because if your income is decoupled from your time, you buy back your life. You gain the freedom to say "Yes" to God without asking a boss for permission.

- **The Employee** asks: "How much can I earn per hour?"

- **The Kingdom Capitalist** asks: "How can I set up a system that frees me to do ministry?"

The Stewardship of Time

We talk often about the stewardship of money, but the stewardship of time is arguably more critical. Ephesians 5:15-16 warns us: *"Look carefully then how you walk, not as unwise but as wise, making the best use of the time, because the days are evil."*

Is it "wise" stewardship to lock 40 to 60 hours of your best energy every week into building someone

else's kingdom, leaving only the scraps of your energy for your family and your faith?

Many believers come home from work exhausted. They have nothing left for their spouse, their kids, or their neighbors. They are "spent." The system is designed to extract maximum value from you, leaving you with just enough to recover on the weekend so you can do it again on Monday.

The Kingdom Capitalist seeks to break this cycle. The goal isn't idleness; it's redeployment. We want to liberate our time from the marketplace so we can invest it in the eternal.

Shifting Your Mindset

Transitioning from an employee mindset to a Kingdom entrepreneur mindset is difficult. It feels risky. But staying in a position where your time is owned by another is also a risk—a risk to your calling.

Here are practical steps to start breaking the constraint:

1. Calculate Your "Freedom Number"
How much money do you actually need to cover your basic living expenses? Not your dream life, but your current life. Once you know that number, you have a target. Your goal is to build side income or business

income that covers that number. Once you hit it, you own your time.

2. Stop "Moonlighting" and Start "Building"

Many people get a second job to pay off debt. That is good for a season. But better than a second job is a side business. A job pays you once. A business pays you repeatedly. If you drive for Uber, you are still trading time for money. If you start a small service business and hire someone else to do the work, you are building an asset.

3. Value Flexibility Over Salary

If you are currently in a job, negotiate for results, not hours. Can you work remotely? Can you condense your work into four days? Fight for flexibility. Every hour you reclaim is an hour you can invest in discipleship, study, or family.

Conclusion

God may call you to a specific job for a specific season to reach specific people. If He has, stay there and be a light! But do not stay there simply because you think it is the only way to survive.

We serve a God of abundance, not scarcity. He did not design you to be a cog in a machine. He designed you to be a leader, a steward, and a creator. It is time to stop asking, "How much time do I have to sell to pay my bills?" and start asking, "What can I build that will pay the bills so I can go serve the Lord?"

Chapter 4: Marketplace Ministry (The "While You Are There" Strategy)

Theme: Using your current employment as a training ground.

It's easy to read the last chapter about the "9-to-5 Constraint" and feel a sense of hopelessness. Maybe you think, "I'm stuck. I have a mortgage, kids in school, and I can't just quit my job to start a business."

If that's you, take a deep breath. This chapter is for you.

The journey to becoming a Kingdom Capitalist doesn't always begin by leaving your job. For many, it begins by revolutionizing how you see your job. Before God calls you to run your own Kingdom-focused business, He first calls you to be a faithful steward in someone else's. Your current workplace is not a waiting room; it is a boot camp. It's the training ground where you learn the skills and forge the character necessary for the next season.

This is the "While You Are There" strategy. While you are in that cubicle, while you are on that factory floor, while you are in that corner office—you are on mission.

Your Unpaid Second Job: Being a Light

Every Christian in the workforce has two jobs. The first is the one on your business card, the one you get paid for. The second, and more important job, is to be an ambassador for Christ.

You may not be able to set your own schedule, but you have something invaluable: access. You have daily access to a group of people who may never step foot inside a church. Your coworkers, your clients, and your vendors are your congregation.

The Apostle Paul gives us the framework for this kind of ministry:

"Whatever you do, work heartily, as for the Lord and not for men, knowing that from the Lord you will receive the inheritance as your reward. You are serving the Lord Christ." (Colossians 3:23-24)

Notice the command: "Work heartily." Your primary act of witness in the workplace is not handing out tracts or arguing about theology. It is being an excellent employee. When you are the most reliable, most diligent, and most honest person on the team, you earn a currency more valuable than money: **Influence.**

Earning the Right to Speak

People don't care what you believe until they believe that you care. In a work context, they won't respect your faith until they respect your work.

Think about the "High-C" employee—the one who is competent, consistent, and has character. When that person speaks, people listen. When that person faces a crisis with peace, people notice. When they are asked to do something unethical and they refuse with grace, they earn a new level of respect.

This is how you build a platform for the Gospel. Your excellence at your job is what gets you the "microphone." Without it, your words are just noise. When you are the best worker in the company, you open doors for ministry that no one else can. Your boss will trust you. Your coworkers will seek your advice. Your character becomes your sermon.

Practical Steps for the In-Job Disciple-Maker

How do you turn this theology into a Monday-to-Friday reality?

1. Practice "Lunchroom Liturgy."
Your lunch break is a sacred hour. Instead of scrolling on your phone, be intentional. Ask a coworker to eat with you. Ask questions about their life, their family, their struggles. Don't go in with a "Gospel presentation" agenda. Go in with a "build a relationship" agenda. Be a good listener. Over time, as trust is built, spiritual conversations will happen naturally.

2. Serve Your Boss.

The Bible tells us to pray for those in authority over us. Your boss is a primary authority figure in your life. Pray for their success. Find ways to make their job easier. When you serve your boss well, you honor God and you gain favor. This doesn't mean being a sycophant; it means having a servant's heart, even toward a difficult leader.

3. Use Your Salary as Seed Capital.

Your current paycheck is not just for paying bills. It is the seed for your future freedom. While you are working your 9-to-5, live on less than you make. Use the margin to do two things:

- **Attack debt:** As we discussed before, debt is a spiritual chain. Use your salary to break it.

- **Invest in your education:** Read books on business, listen to podcasts on investing, and take courses on skills you'll need later. Your current job is funding your transition.

Divine Appointments in the Rhythms of Life

Beyond the lunchroom and the formal meetings, there is a hidden geography to your workday. We often view our commutes, our coffee runs, or our walks to the parking garage as "dead time"—mere transitions from one task to the next. But for the Kingdom Capitalist, these are the **rhythms of life** where God has strategically placed people in your path.

God is the master of the "coincidental" encounter. He has placed the struggling barista at your morning stop, the security guard at the front desk, and the delivery driver who drops off your packages. These people aren't background characters in the story of your career; they are souls in need of a Savior.

To turn these rhythms into ministry, we must master two simple shifts:

- **Take Notice:** We cannot minister to people we don't see. We must train ourselves to look up from our screens and remove our earbuds. Who is the person you see every day but have never spoken to? Who looks burdened in the elevator? Notice the names, the moods, and the small details of those around you.

- **Take Action:** Noticing is the precursor to compassion, but action is the delivery system. Action doesn't have to be a sermon; it can be a sincere "How is your day actually going?", a generous tip, or a simple "I'm going to pray for you" when someone mentions a hardship.

"The steps of a man are established by the Lord, and He delights in his way." (Psalm 37:23)

If God establishes your steps, then the people you bump into throughout your day are not there by accident. They are **divine appointments**. When you view your daily routine through this lens, the mundane becomes electric with spiritual potential. You aren't just "going to work"; you are navigating a mission field that God has specifically designed for you.

The Bridge to What's Next

Your current job is a bridge. For some, it is a bridge to retirement. For the Kingdom Capitalist, it is a bridge to a new level of ministry and impact. You are learning discipline, interacting with different personalities, and seeing how a business operates from the inside.

Do not despise your current position. See it for what it is: a divine appointment. God has placed you there for a reason. You are there to be salt and light. You are there to learn and to grow.

Even if you feel the "9-to-5 Constraint," remember that you are not constrained from praying for your coworkers. You are not constrained from doing your work with excellence. You are not constrained from showing the love of Christ in a tangible way.

Start where you are. Use what you have. The faithfulness you show in your current role is the key that will unlock the door to your next one.

Chapter 5: Passive Income and Radical Flexibility

Theme: Creating systems that work so you can do the Work.

Imagine a scenario: Your church announces an urgent need. A missionary partner in Indonesia has an immediate opening for a team to come and train local pastors for three weeks. It's a critical moment for the church there.

The pastor looks at the congregation and asks, "Who can go?"

In a room of 200 faithful believers, how many hands go up? Usually, very few. It's not because they don't care. It's not because they lack faith. It's because they have jobs. They have bills. They have a boss who won't let them take three weeks off on short notice.

Now, imagine a different reality. Imagine you are sitting in that service. Your bills are paid by rental income from three properties you own. Your business is running smoothly because you have a manager in place. You check your schedule, realize you are free, and your hand shoots up.

This is the power of **Radical Flexibility**.

The Currency of the Kingdom is Time

We often think the most valuable resource we can give to God is our money. While funding the Kingdom is crucial, the most precious asset you possess is your time. Time is the one resource you can never earn back.

Passive income is not about sitting on a beach sipping drinks while money rolls in. That is the world's version of retirement. In the Kingdom, passive income is about decoupling your livelihood from your life's hours so you can redeploy those hours into high-impact ministry.

If you have to work 50 hours a week just to survive, your capacity for discipleship is limited to the margins of your life—nights and weekends. But if your assets cover your living expenses, your entire week becomes available for the Lord's work.

What is Passive Income?

Simply put, active income requires you to be present to earn it (like a salary or hourly wage). Passive income is money earned from assets that you have purchased or created, which continue to pay you with little to no daily effort.

This concept aligns perfectly with the agricultural parables Jesus often used. A farmer works hard to plant a seed (active work). But once the seed is in the ground, "the seed sprouts and grows; he knows not how" (Mark 4:27). The earth produces a crop by itself. The system of nature takes over.

Kingdom Capitalists build "financial orchards." They do the hard work of planting and watering upfront, so they can harvest fruit for years to come.

The "Rich Dad" Principle for the Church

Many of you might be familiar with the concept of making money work for you, popularized by Robert Kiyosaki. While his books focus on financial freedom for personal gain, we must hijack this principle for a higher purpose.

The world says: "Build passive income so you can buy luxury cars and travel endlessly."
The Kingdom says: "Build passive income so you can fund orphanages, mentor young believers, and serve without needing a paycheck."

This is about creating **Margin**. Margin is the space between your load and your limit. When you have financial margin, you have emotional and temporal margin. You can take the call from a hurting friend at 2:00 PM because you aren't clocked in. You can host a small group on Tuesday nights because you aren't working a second shift to pay off debt.

Warning: The Heart Check

There is a danger here. Passive income can easily breed laziness or greed if not submitted to the Lord. The goal is not to escape work; we were created to work. The goal is to escape the *bondage* of working solely for survival.

Before you pursue this path, ask yourself: *"If I didn't have to work for money tomorrow, what would I do with my time?"*

If the answer is "play golf every day," you aren't ready for Kingdom wealth. But if the answer is "I would start a discipleship group for men," or "I would help my church plant a new campus," then you are ready.

Conclusion

God is looking for a people who are free. Free from debt. Free from the fear of lack. Free from the constraints of the time clock.

By building streams of passive income, you are building a reservoir of freedom. You are positioning yourself to be the person who can say "Yes" when the Holy Spirit calls, without having to check with your boss or your bank account first.

Start small. Buy one asset. Create one product. Plant one tree. Over time, that small start can grow into a forest of provision that shelters many.

Chapter 6: Good Debt vs. Bad Debt

Theme: Distinguishing between debt that builds and debt that burdens.

In many churches today, "debt" is often seen as a dirty word. Influenced by well-meaning teachers, many believers view all debt as sinful and something to avoid at all costs. This mindset has led to an approach of extreme financial conservatism, where the ultimate goal is to eliminate debt, save cash, and minimize financial risk.

But is this truly the most effective way to manage resources for God's Kingdom? Could it be that, in our fear of debt, we've overlooked its potential as a tool to further God's work on earth?

Is there a meaningful distinction between *good debt* and *bad debt*?

A Tale of Two Debts

The Bible warns against the dangers of debt. Proverbs 22:7 says, "the borrower is slave to the lender." This is absolutely true when debt is used foolishly.

Bad Debt is the debt that most people are familiar with. It is used to purchase liabilities—things that take money out of your pocket.

- Credit card debt for a vacation you can't afford.

- A car loan for a new vehicle that depreciates the moment you drive it off the lot.

- Financing for consumer goods that satisfy a want, not a need.

This type of debt is driven by materialism and a desire to consume. It creates bondage, increases financial pressure, and limits your ability to be generous. This is the debt that scripture rightfully warns us against. It makes you a slave to the lender and a slave to your possessions.

Good Debt, on the other hand, is a completely different animal. It is debt used to purchase an *asset*—something that puts money *into* your pocket.

- A loan to buy a rental property that generates positive cash flow each month.

- Financing to acquire a profitable business that provides jobs and resources for ministry.

- A loan to expand your own business, allowing you to serve more people and increase your Kingdom impact.

Good debt is an investment. It is using other people's money (the bank's) to acquire a tool that produces more resources than the cost of the debt itself. This isn't slavery; it's smart stewardship.

Has the Church Hoarded Its Talents?

Popular financial teachers like Dave Ramsey have done a great service to the body of Christ by helping countless people escape the bondage of bad debt. The principles of budgeting, living below your means, and avoiding consumer debt are undeniably biblical and wise.

However, a noble mission can have unintended consequences. The widespread "zero debt at all costs" teaching has, in some circles, created a new problem: a culture of hoarding. Believers and churches work diligently to pay off all debt, including their mortgages, and then proceed to pile up cash in savings accounts where it earns next to nothing.

There are mission boards today with tens of millions of dollars sitting in their bank accounts, generating enough interest to fund their entire operations without even touching the principal. While on the surface this might appear to be good stewardship, it highlights a larger issue. Around the world, church planters and missionaries are struggling to secure the resources they need to spread the Gospel and meet the needs of their communities. Many are left begging for financial support just to continue their ministries.

At the root of this disparity, it becomes evident that this is not truly a money problem but a heart problem.

God has blessed His people with an abundance of resources, yet fear, mistrust, or a misaligned understanding of stewardship have led to hoarding rather than giving. It calls for a deeper reflection on what it means to serve God with our finances. Are we storing away treasures on earth out of fear, or are we trusting in God's provision and using His blessings to advance His Kingdom? This is a challenge to align our financial decisions with our faith, ensuring that our resources are actively building the church and supporting those in need.

Think of the parable of the talents. The master rebuked the servant who buried his talent out of fear. He played it safe. He took no risks. And the master called him "wicked and lazy."

Is it possible that by storing up massive cash reserves while missionaries are underfunded and church planters are struggling to make ends meet, we are acting like that fearful servant? We have a world in desperate need, and we are sitting on piles of money, afraid to put it to work.

Having your church building paid off is certainly a good thing—it's a sign of stability and stewardship. But we must remember that it isn't the ultimate goal. The goal is to fill heaven. Having a massive savings account is prudent, but it isn't the mission. The goal is to fund the Great Commission.

The Kingdom Capitalist's Approach to Debt

A Kingdom Capitalist understands that debt is a tool, and like any tool, it can be used for good or for evil. The question is not "Is debt bad?" The question is "What is this debt being used for?"

When you use good debt to buy a cash-flowing asset, you are not increasing your personal burden. You are acquiring a resource-generating engine. The income from that asset pays for the debt and then produces a surplus. That surplus is Kingdom capital. It's money you can use to give generously, support ministry, and buy back your time for discipleship.

This requires wisdom, diligence, and faith. You must learn to analyze deals, understand cash flow, and seek godly counsel. But we must not let fear paralyze us.

A New Mindset

Imagine a church planter who needs $50,000 to launch a new work in an unreached city.

Mindset A (Fear-Based): A church has $500,000 in a savings account. They are afraid of the market and of taking on any risk. They give the planter $5,000 and pray for him, keeping their cash safe.

Mindset B (Faith-Based Stewardship): A Kingdom Capitalist uses $100,000 as a down payment to acquire a $500,000 commercial property that generates $3,000 per month in positive cash flow after all expenses, including the mortgage. They can now fully fund that church planter's $50,000 budget in about a year and a half, and continue funding him year after year from the same asset.

Which mindset better reflects the enterprising spirit of the servants who doubled their master's money?

Conclusion

It's time for the church to mature in its understanding of finance. We must move beyond a simple, one-size-fits-all rule about debt and learn to distinguish between the debt that enslaves and the debt that empowers.

Yes, aggressively pay off your credit cards. Avoid financing depreciating assets. But pray and ask God if He wants you to use the tool of good debt to acquire assets for His glory. Our mission is too critical to be hampered by a fear-based financial theology. The harvest is plentiful, and it needs to be funded.

Chapter 7: Acquisitional Wealth for the Kingdom

Theme: Buying the tools of influence.

There is a romantic notion in the business world about the "startup." We love the story of the entrepreneur in the garage, eating ramen noodles, building something from nothing. While that path is noble, it is also slow, risky, and incredibly difficult. Statistics show that most startups fail within the first five years.

But there is another path—a path often overlooked by believers who want to make an impact in the marketplace. It is the path of **Acquisition**.

Instead of planting a seed and waiting ten years for a tree to grow, what if you just bought the orchard?

This chapter introduces a strategy that might feel foreign to many in the church: *Acquisitional Wealth*. This is the practice of purchasing existing, profitable businesses to steward them for the glory of God.

The "High Ground" Strategy

In military strategy, taking the high ground is essential. It gives you a vantage point and an advantage over the terrain. In the marketplace, established businesses are the "high ground."

When you start a business from scratch, you are at the bottom of the hill fighting your way up. When you *buy* a business, you step onto the high ground immediately.

Imagine purchasing a local HVAC company, a manufacturing plant, or a graphic design firm that has been around for 30 years. On Day One, you have:

- **Cash Flow:** The business is already making money to fund your life and your giving.

- **Customers:** You have hundreds or thousands of people you serve.

- **Employees:** You have a team of people who spend 40 hours a week under your leadership.

- **Reputation:** You have standing in the community.

You are buying a platform. The question is, what will you do with it?

Buying a Culture to Transform It

When a Kingdom Capitalist acquires a business, they are not just buying assets and inventory; they are acquiring a culture. This is where the ministry potential is explosive.

Let's say you buy a local manufacturing shop with 50 employees. Perhaps the previous owner was harsh, the environment was toxic, and the workers felt undervalued.

You walk in as the new owner—a disciple of Jesus. You don't have to preach a sermon in the breakroom to change the atmosphere. You simply start leading like Christ.

- You pay fair wages.
- You treat vendors with honesty.
- You show grace when someone makes a mistake.
- You offer to pray for an employee who is going through a divorce.

Suddenly, the "culture" of that workplace shifts. The toxicity evaporates, replaced by peace and purpose. The employees, who may never step foot in a church, are now swimming in Kingdom values every single day. You have "salted" the earth (Matthew 5:13) simply by signing a purchase agreement.

The Wealth Transfer is Happening Now

Right now, we are in the middle of one of the largest transfers of wealth in history. The "Baby Boomer" generation owns millions of small businesses across the world. As they look to retire, they have a problem: their kids often don't want the business. They want to be YouTubers or doctors; they don't want to run the family plumbing supply company.

This creates a massive opportunity for the church.

If believers do not buy these businesses, who will? Private equity firms? Competitors who care only about the bottom line?

If we want to see our cities transformed, we need believers to step into the gap and acquire these main-street businesses. We need to keep these companies locally owned and Kingdom-focused.

How to Start Thinking Like an Acquirer

You might be thinking, "I don't have millions of dollars to buy a company." Here is the secret: You often don't need your own cash to buy a business.

1. Seller Financing:
Many retiring owners care more about the legacy of their business than getting all the cash upfront. They want to know their employees will be taken care of. Often, they will agree to let you pay them over time using the profits of the business itself.

2. Leveraged Buyouts:
Banks love to lend money for existing businesses with a track record of profit. Unlike a startup, which is a gamble, an existing business has tax returns proving it makes money.

3. Partnerships:

This is where the body of Christ can shine. Maybe you have the skills to run the business, but you lack the capital. There may be another believer in your network who has the capital but lacks the time. By partnering together, you can acquire the asset and share the Kingdom impact.

The Ripple Effect

The goal of Acquisitional Wealth is not to build a personal empire. It is to expand the King's domain.

When a righteous person owns the local car dealership, the single mom doesn't get ripped off on her financing. When a disciple owns the construction company, the contracts are fulfilled with integrity. When a believer owns the tech firm, the profits are used to fight human trafficking or plant churches.

Proverbs 29:2 says, *"When the righteous thrive, the people rejoice; when the wicked rule, the people groan."*

Our communities are groaning. They are tired of greed, corruption, and bad leadership. They are waiting for the righteous to thrive. They are waiting for Kingdom Capitalists to step up, sign the papers, and take the keys.

Practical Steps

- **Look around your town:** What businesses are owned by people who look ready to retire?

- **Search online marketplaces:** Websites like BizBuySell.com and BizQuest.com are excellent platforms for finding businesses for sale in your local area and beyond. These sites allow you to filter by industry, location, and price range, making it easy to find opportunities aligned with your vision.

- **Build your skills:** Learn how to read a balance sheet. Learn the basics of management. Prepare yourself to be a steward.

- **Pray for opportunities:** Ask God, "Is there a business in this city You want me to shepherd?"

Conclusion

Acquisition is an accelerator. It fast-tracks your ability to generate resources and influence people. It is a heavy responsibility, yes. But for the disciple who is grounded in stewardship, it is one of the most effective ways to occupy until He comes.

Chapter 8: Online Businesses: Building Wealth in the Digital Age

Theme: Leveraging the digital world for global impact and personal freedom.

In the parable of the talents, a master entrusts his wealth to his servants. Two of them invest and double the money, earning the master's praise. One servant, however, buries his talent out of fear and is rebuked. The lesson is clear: God expects us to be enterprising with the resources and opportunities He gives us.

In previous chapters, we have discussed traditional business and real estate. But we live in a unique moment in history. Never before has it been possible to build a global business from a laptop in your living room. The internet has created a new frontier for the Kingdom Capitalist, and we are called to be faithful stewards of this powerful tool.

This is the age of the online business, a vehicle that offers unprecedented scalability, flexibility, and global reach for the cause of Christ.

The Digital Great Commission

The internet has flattened the world. With an online business, your "local market" is the entire English-speaking world, or Spanish-speaking world, or whatever group you are called to serve. Your potential customer base is not limited by geography.

This is a game-changer for Kingdom impact.

- An e-commerce store selling 30-day consumable products like coffee, supplements, or toothpaste can generate a recurring, passive income stream through subscriptions, fueling efforts to support Kingdom work.

- A digital subscription box with curated high-quality items like specialty coffee, self-care products, or practical tools can inspire and equip thousands, all while creating a sustainable profit stream for Kingdom impact.

The digital space is not a distraction from "real" ministry; it is one of the most strategic mission fields of our generation. It allows us to fulfill the Great Commission by going into all the world, digitally.

Why Online Business is a Kingdom Accelerator

As many successful online entrepreneurs have discovered, the digital marketplace offers unique advantages for those seeking to build wealth for the Kingdom.

1. Low Startup Costs:
Unlike a brick-and-mortar business that requires a

physical location and massive upfront investment, many online businesses can be started with very little capital. You can build a website for a few hundred dollars and start selling digital products or services immediately. This lowers the barrier to entry, allowing more believers to step into entrepreneurship.

2. Scalability:

If you sell physical products, like supplements, you don't have to manufacture or ship them yourself. With third-party vendors, your products can be stored, packaged, and shipped on your behalf. This means you don't need to carry inventory, hire employees, or handle logistics. This model offers incredible time flexibility and scalability, allowing your business to grow without tying up your time.

3. Unmatched Flexibility:

An online business can often be run from anywhere with an internet connection. This provides the radical flexibility we discussed earlier. It means you can travel for a mission trip while still managing your business. It means you can be present for your family while still generating an income. You are no longer tethered to a physical location.

Practical Models for Digital Kingdom Builders

There are countless ways to build a business online. Here are a few models that are particularly well-suited for Kingdom Capitalists:

1. E-commerce: This involves selling physical products online. You might create your own brand of products, or you could use a model like "print-on-demand" to sell custom-designed t-shirts, mugs, and other items without ever touching the inventory yourself..

2. Affiliate Marketing: This is the practice of recommending other people's products and earning a commission on any sales that result from your referral. If you have a blog, podcast, or social media following, you can monetize your platform by recommending products and services that you trust and that align with your values.

3. Network Marketing: While not all network marketing companies are created equal, finding the right one can be highly profitable without being pushy or "salesy." This model allows you to earn income by sharing products you genuinely love and believe in, while building a team of like-minded individuals who do the same. Best of all, you can succeed in this space while fully maintaining your character and integrity, using it as a powerful vehicle for creating residual income and community through honest service.

The Mindset is Key

As you explore the world of online business, the principles remain the same. The goal is not just to get rich. The goal is to build wealth *now* so you can do more for the Kingdom.

- **Serve First:** Your primary aim must be to solve a problem or meet a need for your customers. Profit is the byproduct of excellent service.

- **Maintain Integrity:** The internet can feel anonymous, making it tempting to cut corners. As a believer, your online business must be a beacon of honesty and integrity.

- **Invest in Yourself:** The digital world changes quickly. You must be committed to learning new skills, whether it's marketing, technology, or finance. Your business will only grow to the extent that you do.

Conclusion

The digital age is not something to be feared; it is an opportunity to be seized. God has given our generation a tool that the Apostle Paul could only have dreamed of. We can reach more people, more quickly, and more cost-effectively than ever before.

By building an online business, you are not just creating financial freedom for yourself. You are building a wealth-generating engine that can fund missions, support your local church, and free up your time to make disciples. You are taking the "talent" God has given you and putting it to work for an eternal return.

Chapter 9: The Kingdom Budget: Aligning Your Finances with Your Mission

Theme: Your budget reveals your heart. Make sure it has a Kingdom pulse.

Where does your money go? If someone examined your bank statement or family budget, what story would it tell? Budgets are not just numbers and spreadsheets; they reveal our priorities with brutal honesty. As Jesus said, "For where your treasure is, there your heart will be also" (Matthew 6:21).

We can talk endlessly about our passion for the Great Commission and our desire to see the lost saved. But if that mission doesn't show up in our financial plans, our words are empty. If the Great Commission is truly our goal, it should have a place in our budget—both as individuals and as churches.

The Prayer List Problem

Often, you don't need to review a church's budget to see where its priorities lie. Just look at the prayer list. Week after week, these lists are filled with requests for physical healing—prayers for Aunt Sally's knee surgery or Brother John's cancer treatment. These prayers are important and necessary.

But where are the prayers for our spiritually lost neighbors? Where is the desperate intercession for the coworker who doesn't know Christ and is heading for an eternity without Him? The imbalance is telling. Too often, we are more concerned with temporary struggles than with eternal destinies.

Jesus demonstrated the eternal value of a soul through His sacrifice on the cross. God sent His only Son not just to heal physical ailments but to rescue humanity from sin and eternal separation. Yet, how often are we more focused on someone's health than their salvation? Yes, praying for healing is important, but even if someone recovers, their body will still perish one day. What truly matters is their eternity. Shouldn't our first and most fervent prayer be for their salvation? Let's align our hearts with God's priority—to seek and save the lost—and pray earnestly for those who need the eternal hope only Christ can provide.

Our focus on physical comfort over spiritual urgency exposes a deeper heart issue. That issue inevitably shows up in how we spend our time and money. If the lost aren't part of our prayer list, they likely aren't part of our budget either.

The Luke 16:9 Principle

In Luke 16:9, Jesus gives a striking command after the parable of the shrewd manager: "I tell you, use worldly wealth to gain friends for yourselves, so that when it is gone, you will be welcomed into eternal dwellings."

He instructs us to use "unrighteous mammon"—earthly money—for eternal purposes. We are called to leverage our finances to introduce people to Jesus, turning them into "friends" who will welcome us in heaven. This isn't a suggestion; it's a strategy for every believer.

I have a friend, Devin, whom I met when I hired him to build a fence. Over the week he worked on the project, I had several chances to build a relationship with him. By the end of the week, our conversations shifted from surface-level topics to deeper, spiritual discussions. I suggested starting a Bible study together, and to my surprise, he agreed. For months, we met weekly at Chick-fil-A, where I paid for his meal each time. Those conversations became life-changing, and eventually, Devin put his faith in the Lord. That experience reminded me of what it means to live out Kingdom values—using the resources God has entrusted to us to build relationships, share the Gospel, and make an eternal impact.

How can we apply this? Create a specific "Luke 16:9" line item in your budget. This isn't for tithes or regular offerings but for relational evangelism—money set aside to connect with the lost, build bridges, and share the Gospel.

Let's reflect God's priorities not just in our hearts but in our actions, our prayers, and yes, even in our budgets. Eternity is at stake.

What does this look like?

- **Joining a gym or a hobby class** not just for personal benefit, but with the expressed purpose of meeting and building relationships with non-believers.

- **Budgeting to take a coworker or neighbor to lunch** once a week, creating space to listen to their story and share yours.

- **Setting aside money to host people for dinner,** practicing hospitality and showing the love of Christ in a tangible way.

- **Having a fund to help a non-believing friend** in a moment of crisis, demonstrating the generosity of the Kingdom without expectation.

This is not just "spending money." This is strategic, mission-driven investment. It is using your wealth, whether it is a little or a lot, to create opportunities for the Gospel.

One of my weekly routines is playing pick-up basketball with the same group of guys. On the surface, it's just friendly competition—a chance to work up a sweat and enjoy the game. But for me, it's more than that. I make it a habit to pray for these guys throughout the week—for their lives, their struggles, and their hearts. Over time, we've built relationships that go beyond the court. We laugh, share stories, and support each other in meaningful ways. Basketball is fun, but what makes it truly fulfilling is the deeper purpose it serves. Through these relationships, I have the chance to reflect Christ's love, turning each game into an opportunity to plant seeds for the Kingdom.

The Church's Luke 16:9 Budget

Church budgets often reveal where priorities lie, and it's disheartening to see that many allocate little to no resources for local missions, church planting, or community outreach. A line item for Luke 16:9, a verse that calls believers to make friends for eternal purposes through the stewardship of worldly resources, should be central to every church's financial plan. Sadly, while some churches possess budgets stretching into the hundreds of thousands or even millions, these funds are often aimed at building larger, more extravagant facilities rather than expanding the Kingdom through outreach and church planting.

Imagine the transformation if these churches shifted their focus from "building and building" to "sending and planting." By equipping and sending faithful disciples to plant new churches, the Gospel can reach untapped communities and foster revival in areas desperately in need of hope. This is true Kingdom impact—investing in what lasts for eternity, rather than earthly structures. Churches that prioritize Kingdom-focused stewardship can fulfill their call to make disciples in every corner, showing the world what it truly means to live with a mission-driven faith.

From Kingdom Talk to Kingdom Walk

We know that we should have a Kingdom focus. We sing about it and we talk about it. But our actions, and specifically our budgets, must demonstrate that Kingdom drive.

A budget with a Luke 16:9 line item is a declaration of intent. It says, "My life is not just about paying bills and saving for retirement. My life is about seeing people meet Jesus, and I am willing to fund that mission personally."

It transforms your financial planning from a defensive exercise of managing scarcity into an offensive strategy for Kingdom advance. It forces you to ask questions like, "Who is God calling me to invest in this month?" and "How can I use these resources to open a door for the Gospel?"

This is the essence of being a Kingdom Capitalist. It's not just about building wealth, but about deploying it with wisdom and purpose. Start today. Open your budget, and before you allocate money for subscriptions, entertainment, or even savings, create a line item for eternity. Let your budget show the world—and remind yourself—what your heart treasures most.

Chapter 10: The Multiplication Mandate (Real-Life Discipleship)

Theme: The end goal is always people.

We have spent several chapters talking about money, business, real estate, and online income. We have discussed systems, assets, and acquisition. But if we stop there, we have failed.

If you build a massive business empire, achieve total financial freedom, and retire early, but do not make disciples, you have not succeeded as a Kingdom Capitalist. You have merely succeeded as a capitalist.

The Bible calls wealth without purpose "vanity." It is a chasing after the wind. The only thing you can take with you from this life to the next is not your portfolio, your brand, or your real estate deeds. The only thing you can take to heaven is *people*.

This final chapter brings us back to the heart of the matter. Why do we do all of this? Why do we fight to get out of debt? Why do we build businesses? Why do we seek passive income?

We do it to fulfill the Multiplication Mandate.

The ROI of Souls

In business, we measure ROI (Return on Investment). In the Kingdom, the currency is different. The currency is souls.

The Great Commission in Matthew 28:19 is not a suggestion; it is a command: "Go therefore and make disciples of all nations."

For the Kingdom Capitalist, our assets are simply the tools we use to obey this command.

- We use our **businesses** to find the lost—hiring those who need a second chance, serving customers with grace, and modeling integrity in a corrupt marketplace.

- We use our **passive income** to feed the hungry and train the willing—funding the seminaries, the orphanages, and the church plants that others cannot afford to support.

- We use our **flexibility** to walk alongside the broken—having the time freedom to mentor a young father, visit the sick, or lead a small group without being exhausted from a 60-hour work week.

When we view our resources through this lens, every dollar becomes a seed for the gospel. Every hour of freedom becomes an opportunity for ministry.

Moving from "Spiritually Dead" to "Spiritual Parent"

Real-life discipleship is a process. It involves helping people move from being spiritually dead (unbelievers) to being spiritual infants (new believers), then spiritual children (growing believers), then spiritual young adults (serving believers), and finally spiritual parents (disciple-makers).

Most people get stuck because they lack the time or resources to invest in others.

But you—the Kingdom Capitalist—are building a life designed for investment. You are positioning yourself to be a spiritual parent. You are clearing the clutter from your schedule so you can sit across the table from someone and help them grow.

This is the "Kingdom Multiplier" effect we discussed in the introduction. When you disciple someone, and they go on to disciple others, your impact outlives you. You are not just adding to the Kingdom; you are multiplying it.

The Ultimate Performance Review

One day, every single one of us will stand before the King. It will be the ultimate performance review.

On that day, Jesus will not ask to see your balance sheet. He will not be impressed by your market share or your follower count. He will look at how you stewarded what He gave you.

The goal of the Kingdom Capitalist is to hear those six words: **"Well done, good and faithful servant."**

We want to hear that not because we accumulated the most gold, but because we used the "unrighteous mammon" of this world to populate heaven. We want to look around in eternity and see faces—people who are there because we funded the mission that reached them, or because we had the time to share the Gospel with them.

That is the only legacy that matters.

Conclusion: Start Where You Are

The journey from an employee mindset to a Kingdom Capitalist mindset does not happen overnight. It is a process of renewing your mind and disciplining your habits.

You might be reading this and feeling overwhelmed. You might be deep in debt, working a job you dislike, with zero assets to your name.

Do not be discouraged. Start where you are.

You do not need to wait until you are a millionaire to be a Kingdom Capitalist. You can start today with the widow's mite. You can start today by being faithful with the little you have.

Commit to the instruction found in 1 Timothy 6:18:

"Command them to do good, to be rich in good deeds, and to be generous and willing to share."

Notice that Paul tells Timothy to command the rich to be rich in *good deeds*, not just money.

Whether you are in a cubicle, on a construction site, or in a corner office, the mission is the same: Make Disciples. The tool is simply different.

God has placed you in this time and this economy for a reason. He has given you the ability to produce wealth (Deuteronomy 8:18) to confirm His covenant.

So, go. Build businesses. Crush debt. Invest wisely.
Buy back your time.
But do it all with one eye on eternity.

The harvest is plentiful, and the laborers are few. It is time for the laborers to get to work.

At the end of the day, it is not a money problem; it is a heart problem.

www.ingramcontent.com/pod-product-compliance
Lightning Source LLC
LaVergne TN
LVHW051429080426
835508LV00022B/3319